The Cheetah

and

the

Patricia Furstenberg

Print Edition ISBN 9781973208532
Version: 2019-01-07
First print edition 2017
Cover Design: Marcus & Patricia Furstenberg
Independently Published

Other books by Patricia Furstenberg

From the same series:
The Elephant and the Sheep
The Lion and the Dog

Africa's Bravest Creatures series:
Jock of the Bushveld
Huberta the Hippo
Vonk the Horse

Joyful Trouble
As Good as Gold
Happy Friends
Puppy, 12 Months of Rhymes and Smiles
Belle Cat

Connect with the author on Twitter: @PatFurstenberg
Author's website: www.alluringcreations.co.za/wp

To my Father

Table of Contents:

This poem was inspired by the real life story of Kasi, an orphaned male cheetah, and Mtani, a female Labrador, which struck a remarkable friendship and remained life-long friends... in Africa.

Two wet noses met one day,

Quite by chance, each one on a trail.

The sun was high, the day was hot,

When dust blew up you could see not.

Such are Africa's wild plains,

With long, hot summers and tails with tales.

One had spots and an agile body;

The other, gold fur and was rather chubby.

Yet they both loved the chase and to hide in the dust;

Hide, seek, wait, pounce, your instinct trust.

And while they ran, having so much fun,

Their own pray, rabbit, was soon... gone!

The Cheetah and the Dog

Leaving the game, the dust and the sun;

Saving his skin and his fur. What a run!

The hare never stopped till he reached his home,

He hid beneath his bed with a shiver and a groan.

He never left his bush again, the rabbit kept away

From the dry, hot plains where two tails played.

The two busy bodies enjoyed the chase,

One after the other's tail, all over the place;

Is it mine or yours? What a fun of a hunt!

Now I'm ahead, while you stop to pant.

Hunting something small can become a bore;

Find someone like you, who loves to play and explore.

"That rabbit was slow," purred one as she stretched.

"TOO FAST," howled the other while in dust he laid.

"I'd rather chase something big, like you," cheetah said

And, like any cat, jumped a tree for shed.

The dog barked once, caught a fly, then sneezed

And, like any dog, closed his eyes, looking pleased.

The sun was up, the day long ahead;

No worries in the world, so they barked, purred and slept.

Up from their nap, in the cool evening air,

Two pointy ears with one long tail

Chased the flopping ones with the wiggly end.

Forward and sideways, fun to catch a friend!

And when round bottomed one bounced about,

The long legged one chose to leap around.

When the long legged creature jumped a tree and lied low,

The soft bottomed one waited patiently below.

Panting, "My turn to chase," the dog soon said

As he dashed after cheetah and her purring head.

Taking shortcuts, stooping low,

Jumping from behind, "Hello!"

A cheetah and a dog,

Playing by the log?

"Stay away from that spot-less one," the cheetah was told.

Yet the two had fun; they did nothing wrong.

"Beware, or the spotty-one will hunt you," heard the dog.

Yet they kept on playing down the road, by their log.

Chasing each other under African sun;

Barking, purring; having fun.

And "the one with the speed" as cheetah was known,

Or Kasi, for short, as she was often called,

And "close friend", or Mtani the dog,

Shared even some meat and a bone, by their log.

Year after year Kasi slowed her pace,

Allowing friend Mtani to catch up in their race;

For a race between friends is only fun

If both of them win and both keep the pace.

And Mtani taught Kasi a thing or two

About tasty veld plants, grass too.

One late day in summer, as they lazily napped,

Kasi on her branch, Mtani's ears flapped.

The dog's picked up a sudden tremor in the ground,

Rumblings, voices, the humans were around!

Kasi only watched as she lazily stretched,

But Mtani knew their talk: DANGER it spelled!

The dog warned Kasi and the whole cheetah clan;

"The humans have weapons; they'll hunt you, old and young."

So cheetahs fled in time, saving their spots

And thanked their new friend, Mtani, lots and lots.

Mtani wagged his tail like any dog would

And the cheetah cubs did the same, for sure!

The sun was up, the summer stretched ahead;

The cheetahs welcomed Mtani as their friend.

Now one winter day, when food was scarce,

Mtani brought a bone to share between friends.

Two lionesses smelled food, stalked their prey:

"Here's lunch," hummed one. The other puffed, "Child's play!"

Mtani whimpered, backed away to the tree. "Trapped!"

"No one hunts MY friend," above him, cheetah hissed.

The dog was saved and that night, it is said,

A cheetah joined his pack and food they shared.

And no one understood how no dog even barked

When a cheetah came to farm, one night in the past.

But you know why, don't you?

Cheetah and dog were friends, through and through.

This story is true and it is often told

To all in Africa, young and old.

Friendship has no boundaries, friendship is fun,

It cares not about your colour or how fast you can run.

Friends help each other, friends laugh and share.

So be like cheetah and dog, just smile and care.

Amazing Cheetah Facts

Today there are less and less cheetahs living in the wild; we say that the number of cheetahs is **decreasing** and that the population of cheetah is **vulnerable**.

Cheetahs are Africa's most **endangered** big cat.

There are about **7 100 cheetah**s left in the world today, living freely and happily in the wild or in nature reserves.

Why do cheetahs need to live in the wild?

Part of the way cheetahs hunt is instinctive, but a lot is learned from their mother.

Cheetah cubs hunt with their mother between 8 weeks and 14 months.

The cheetah mother will hunt and wound the

prey, then release it for her cubs to have a turn at catching it. If they don't, she will catch the prey and release it again for them to hunt, thus giving them another chance to learn.

Example 1: a cheetah that was born and raised in captivity, when released in the wild would hunt smaller giraffes. This happens because the cheetah would hunt based on her instinct alone. A cheetah growing in the wild would learn from her mother to hunt a bigger prey.

Example 2: a cheetah that was born and raised in captivity, when released in the wild was seen to try to attack a buffalo. This is all wrong because the cheetahs jaw and teeth cannot handle such a big prey.

Why should cheetahs hunt a bigger prey?

Cheetahs burn a lot of energy when hunting, so they cannot hunt for a long time. They need a big meal to refill themselves and feed their cubs. A mother cheetah can have between 2 and 8 cubs living with her.

Hunting a mature animal, a giraffe for example, will give the younger giraffe time to grow and have her own babies, this way increasing the number of giraffes and helping to protect the giraffe population.

How were cheetahs built to live in the wild.

Cheetahs are the **fastest animal on land**: they can go from a dead standstill to sixty miles per hour - or 96 kilometers per hour - in 3 seconds.

Cheetahs can run this fast because their skeleton is flexible and it allows their backbone to curve up and down when they runs. This helps their legs move faster and their stride (lengths between steps) to be longer.

Cheetahs can run this fast for about 10 football fields in lengths or 1kilometer before they overheat and must stop.

If they don't stop from their run their bodies will need to burn more calories to make more energy to help them run, but with the energy comes heat as well. So they will overheat and die.

When they run this fast their stride is 6-7 meters long (21 feet).

Cheetahs body is designed for running fast: their head is small, their chest is wide, their legs are long. Their tail is heavy and long, helping them balance and acts as a rudder when they chase the prey.

Cheetahs have small teeth to make room for their large nostrils. They need these to breath enough air when chasing their prey.

Cheetahs are not like other cats: they hunt by day, they like fresh meat.

Cheetahs have semi non-retractable claws, almost like dog claws. Their claws help them when they run, like the spikes on a footballer's shoes. The pads on their feet are not soft, like those of most cats, but hard like a rubber, helping them grip the ground when they run.

Because they hunt during daytime, the fur on the inside corner of their eyes has two black lines, "tear lines", to reflect the glare of the sun. Just like the black marks that football players put under their eyes during the games.

For the first three months cheetah cubs have long, grey fur on their heads, shoulders and back to help them camouflage (disguise) in the long grass where they live.

More books in this collection:

The Elephant and the Sheep

The Lion and the Dog

More books by the same author:

About the Author:

Patricia Furstenberg is a skilled children's book author, poetess and mother, known for her uplifting, charming themes and lovable, enchanting characters: dogs, cats, elephants, cheetahs, lions, but also squirrels and snails. Her words "truly make the world a happier and more beautiful place!".

Her book "Joyful Trouble" is an Amazon Bestseller. Her book of poems "As Good As Gold" became a #1 New Release the day it was published.

Find more of Patricia's stories on her author page,

Alluring Creations, http://alluringcreations.co.za/wp/

Made in the USA
Coppell, TX
19 December 2019

13357066R00024